Doxology of Nonlocality

Cuffee the Magnificent

DEDICATION

Mom & Dad

CONTENTS

ACKNOWLEDGMENTS

I thank God for giving me a spirit of creativity.

I thank my family and friends for their encouragement.

I thank you, the reader, for supporting my work.

GLORY

We march
Hand and foot
Side by side
Brothers in Arms

They command us
The orders come down from the monarchy
From his ivory tower
His palace
He gives us orders

But he does not stand here!
On this ground of blood
He does not stand here!
And have to look face to face
With another man while you cut

He doesn't stand here
And take a life
Again and again
In the name of an order

They say that it's for glory
They say it's for honor and duty

I say it's for greed!

For I have fought in the name of my country
I have fought in the name of my sovereign
And I have fought in the name of God

And the only glory I have seen
Is the glory leaving a man's body
As he falls to the ground
At my hand
Before my feet

So don't tell me that it's for honor!
Don't tell me that it's for justice and peace!

I am done with this!

If I will fight
If I will raise my weapon
And my sword
If I will run my spear
Through another man's spine

If I will ever take another life
It will be to protect my family

It will be for love
It will be for security
It will be for passion

So what will I do now?

LIBERTY

In the heat of battle

In the morning of the day

In the garden of the dead

In the winter of May

I can not continue to do this

I will not continue

To do what I am told

To not think

To not follow my heart

And to forsake everything that is dear to me

Today is the day!

And now is the time!

I will not let another day go by
Living like this!

Killing!
Hurting!
Destroying!
For another man's treasure!

So I throw down my armor
And take off my helmet
You can have my sword
You can take my shield

Here is my spear
And here are my boots

You can no longer call me
Soldier

Because

I am a man

I am a husband

I am a father

I am a brother

I am an uncle

I am a son

That comes first

So you will never see me again

I am not afraid of the darkness that waits before me

I am not afraid of the journey that I will have to take

Because nothing can stop me!

No one can stop me!

Because I have faith in my ability to adapt

And position myself for success!

There is no obstacle that can come my way

There is no circumstance that can stand before me

There is no mountain

No fire

No ocean

That will prevent me from living my life

There is no man

There is no sovereign

There is no idol

That will make me bow

I can see my liberty

Through those gates

SUN

"This is treason"
He said to me

He did not understand
What would make a general
A commander
With so much potential
Turn his face
Against his king

I said to him
"You are but a man
A man just like I am
Your wife is but a woman
A woman just like my wife

You are not gods
You are not supernatural
You are not angels
You are not demons

You are human
Just like I am"

He interrupted me
As he threw down his cup of crimson wine
"You subordinate!
You slave!
You are nothing without me!
I am your king!"

As the wine stained and blood was in the floor
I said
"I have no king
But the Sun
And I will bow my knees to no one

But to that Great Star
That shines down on us all

If that is treason
Then I am guilty
But how can you punish me
When I don't belong to you?
The only one that can judge me
Sits on the throne of my heart

I turned around
To leave his court
And his guards
Chained me
Suffocated me
Until all was darkness

Then I opened my eyes
In hell

DARKNESS

There was no fire

There was no screaming

No demons

No souls

It was just me

Standing in the darkness

I asked myself

"Is this my punishment

For all the lives that I have taken

In the name of my sovereign?

Is there no forgiveness

For a man like me?"

I tried to do everything right

Everyone told me to enlist

So I joined

They praised me for being a good soldier

I was reward

I was awarded

Tribute and honor

And praise

For my skill

For my talent

To bring death

I was worshiped

The king himself knew my name

My family was proud of me

My mother and father

Looked on me with pride

That I carried their name

That I was their son

I tried to do everything right
In the eyes of everyone
Is this
My punishment

From the darkness
He said
"Son,
This isn't hell

Arise"

ANOINTED

From the darkness

From the void

From uncertainty

An old man

A full beard

Long hair

Shackles on his feet

And on his hands

We were incarcerated

I said

"I didn't see you there

Where did you come from?

Who are you?"

He said to me

"I was like you when I was young

I followed all the rules

I did everything I thought was expected of me

But look at me

It's been 20 years

And I have never left this cell"

I asked him

"What is your name?

What did you do to deserve such a punishment?"

He said

"It's been so long

I don't even know my own name

The guards call me Nobody

They call me Slave

They call me a Waste of Space

And when they bring me food

They say

I am stealing from the dogs

And it would be better if given to pigs"

Again I asked

"What did you do?"

He said

"It's been so long

I don't even remember

The guards tell me that I killed someone

They tell me that I murdered someone

Someone important

They say that I lied and deceived

But I don't remember

I don't remember

I don't remember who I am

Or what I've done"

I backed away from him

I did not want that to be me in 20 years
I did not want to look back and see
And not remember
To only have my legacy and history
Anointed to be
By heartless prison guards

I bowed my head
That will not be me
I stood tall instead
That will not be me

I will live
I will have my liberty

A key
A door
A guard
On the floor

Knocked down

Dragged out the cell

Three commanded me

"You are young

We can use you to fight"

SLAVE

They marched me through

Through the halls of this dungeon

And the faint sound of cheering

Grew louder and louder still

Corridors until

We were in open yard

A crowd

Prison guards

Gamblers

Even soldiers that I once commanded

All gathered around a fight

Fighting to the death

So the audience could make money

Betting on us like dogs

Treating us

Dehumanizing us

Holding me by the neck

The guard roared

"You're next!

Whoever wins this fight

Will be your devil"

Once the blood was too much

The internal scars

Far too much

One man was dead

The other stood motionless

Not with pride

Not celebrating a victory

But like cattle

Thankful that the butcher was late

They threw me in
Told me to fight
"You'll die in here anyway
So why not die fighting"
They reasoned

"If you don't fight
We'll kill you"
They promised

I said to my opponent
"My brother
We don't have to do this"

He said to me with eyes of distress
Tears of hopelessness
"Yes we do
We are slaves now"

I said to him

"My brother

You are no slave

You are no slave

I'm sure that just like me

You are innocent

But they told you that you were guilty

They told you that you did something wrong

But I can see it in your eyes

That you are not a criminal

You do not deserve to be in here

Nor do I"

A blow to my chest

A kick to my side

"Enough talking"

The guard said

I want to see fighting instead"

So my opponent

Running toward me

Pressed a force of a foot

On my neck

LIE

I grabbed my throat

Trying to catch my breath

Preventing me from suffocating

To death

Rolling on the floor

I reached out again

"My brother

We don't have to do this"

But his hand pressed upon my flesh

The bone in my rib was no more

Again I pleaded

"We are innocent men!

In an unfair game!

But if we don't play
Then we can rise above this"

A force in my right eye
My sight was taken from me

And I confessed
"My brother
I would rather die
Then to live a lie
I would rather stand here
With no defense
If it will set your mind free"

He said to me
"But we have to do this?"

I replied
"No we don't"

He looked at the body of the man
That he killed before
He looked at me and my bruises
I image that he foresaw
The emotion
Of my dead body

At that moment
He fell to his knees
Said he
"I am done!"

The guards said
"If you will not fight
Then we will torture you
Until you do"

In a moment of a moment
They tied our hands behind our backs

Pulled out knives

Heated metal

Hot coals

Pots of boiling water

TRUTH

It was soon to begin

A time of torture

A point of pain

There was no way for me

And my mind to prepare

All I knew was that I would not be

Dehumanized

What would my son say

If I bowed my knee

To ignorance?

To selfishness?

If I bow my knee

If I give in

What would be the legacy?
What would be the heritage?

I would rather take this pain
I would rather die
Mutilated
Disfigured

Then to live
Without my humanity
Without my dignity

If I don't make it out alive
If today is my last day

Let it be said
To my son
And to my son's sons

I stood for Righteousness

I stood for Truth

I stood for the Sun

I stood for Love

ABOUT THE AUTHOR

Cuffee the Magnificent is a musician and poet that ignites a passion for life and truth in the hearts of audiences around the world.

www.CuffeeMagnificent.com

ADDITIONAL WORKS

Poetry

Riddle of Life

Music

Riddle of Life
A Musical Interpretation

Doxology of Nonlocality
A Musical Interpretation

www.ingramcontent.com/pod-product-compliance
Lightning Source LLC
Chambersburg PA
CBHW030310030426
42337CB00012B/665